TO

THANK YOU NOW
ENJOY

A CRIER'S RHYMES

STAN

A CRIER'S RHYMES

Have a read, have a laugh, some are just plane daft

STANLEY WHITCHER

To order additional copies of this book, contact:
Xlibris
800-056-3182
www.Xlibrispublishing.co.uk
Orders@Xlibrispublishing.co.uk
803966

Editor's note:

I have taken the liberty of correcting some of Stan's spelling errors and typos. I've left in spelling mistakes which might have been deliberate. Most of the remaining errors will be words that I've mis-spelled, or just plain missed by my spelling checker, which doesn't know the difference between "it's", "its" and perhaps "its'". Please report serious errors to steve.j.swift@gmail.com

Contents

A day of rest

As I lay they're in my bed and hear the tattle tittle
Of all the ladies all around yes I'm in hospital
They don't know what's wrong with me but they've done some tests
They've stuck another needle in along with all the rest

They've pulled and prodded on my chest and done a full x ray
And then they said turn over, no, no the other way
I thought oh no what is it now? He's going to do to me
I shut my eyes and held my breath but all he said was gee

Well I think that's all for now you go back to the unit
And be careful with that gown on, it's quite easy to moon it
So I got back to the unit with apprehension some
I didn't want embarrassment and the ladies see my bum

But it all turned out ok and I felt a little tired
They said before you go to sleep you have to be rewired
And then they stuck these little things all over my chest
The lights came on in gadgets they said now you get some rest

But I am fascinated by the lights upon a screen
They were my illuminations the first ones I had seen
But they were all nice and steady as if done just to please
All these flipping gadgets marvellous those Japanese

Oh no here comes the nurse what is she up to now
She says she wants my blood pressure and maybe mops my brow
I ask have you got my test results? She says maybe in a week
I say oh my bleeding giddy aunt can l now get some sleep.

A dog's life

Now I'm a dog, a mongrel dog, with a human as my master
He has two legs I have four and I can run the faster
He is tall and I am short, hardly to his knees
If you're not sure which one is me, I'm the one with fleas

I do try to get rid of them, I roll upon the grass
He does too when we get home he sticks me in the bath
He sprays me down to get me clean, but if he gets a call
I take the opportunity to shake it up the wall

I scramble out, he towels me down, and my coat is all a fluff
I don't know why he bothers, perhaps he's entered me at Crufts
To work I haven't got to, I really think he's thick
All I ever seem to do is bring him back a stick

And when I pooh he picks it up and saves it in a bin
I tell you now I wouldn't do the same for him
Yes he takes me walks and throws the stick then puts me on the lead
Then takes me home and gives me water and an appetising feed

Then I just lay there panting or I maybe tease the cat
Now I really couldn't have a life much easier than that
I suppose he only keeps me because he needs a friend
But he can't bark, and I can't talk, so it's all a bit pretend

So as a dog I'll tell you now, and if I could I'd bet
You wouldn't catch a dog having a human for a pet.

A Reindeer

Now if I was a reindeer around this time of year
I'd make myself look pretty scarce, pretend I wasn't here
I'd go into the forest, not see the light of day
I don't want to be the one that has to pull that heavy sleigh

You may think it's very cute upon your Christmas cards
But when you think about the job it must be very hard
You see the reindeer pull the sleigh right across the sky
Now I've learnt quite a lot in life but I don't know how to fly

And just how do you park the thing on every flipping roof
I haven't got big plates of meat, only four small hoof
And all those presents piled high with Santa on the back
all dressed up in red and white plus his great big sack

He must put in some practice, and practice quite a lot
How does he get his great big girth down a nine inch chimney pot?
He really must have magic which no one yet has seen
I mean he goes down sooty chimneys, and comes up squeaky clean.

And how would I take off again? We must be gone by sun up
I wouldn't even have a decent reindeer run up
Oh There must be other reindeer much more qualified than me
so I, l just stand back and wish you well
around your Christmas tree.

A thought

A thought took shape in this man's head
As he lay there on his bed
He knew not why he thought of it
He wasn't brainy more like a twit

He grabbed a pencil and some paper
Then he started to design this caper
He drew circles squares and angles
It looked like something quite new fangled

At one end it had he added a point
You couldn't even see the joint
He was going to make it out of tin
Then even put a doorway in

Then having started with his fun
He then put in another one
Many things he drew aboard
Everything he could afford

The look of joy upon his face
When he thought to build a base
So he had one built at ten foot high
When built put me on it to face the sky

What I was then and I could bet
Because in my base he put a jet
I didn't know my destination
But I looked up with trepidation

Yes a spaceship that is me
Once sent bound for eternity
One thing my insides sure did lack
Was any means to bring me back

So if you look up from below
And think you see a UFO
Just think again at what you spied
I've yet to be identified

I'm way up high it's oh so far
You could be looking at a star
Way out in space I've lost my jet
So that's the end I don't know where I'll get.

A tickle itch

If I had a choice in life of something else to be
I might become an irritant, something like a flea
Because they are small and tiny and hard to ferret out
They make you itch and make you scratch as they hop about

But thinking about other things I've now decided which
I won't become the little flea, I shall just become the itch
An itch of course you cannot see, and so you cannot kill
There is no doubt about it to scratch you surely will

I would get in awkward places like the middle of your back
You would have to find an instrument to launch a scratch attack
And when you've had a good old scratch, and forced me to retreat
I would find another place to itch, to embarrass you in the street

I would itch in places too embarrassing to scratch
People would steer clear of you for fear what they might catch
I would have such fun with you and not cause any pain
You'd scratch me here and scratch me
there and scratch me once again

You'd have no control you see I would be in charge
Because I can be a little itch, ore I can be one large
And every time you scratch my mission would be complete
I would chuckle when you scratched like
mad when walking down the street

A Toast

I'll drink a toast, a thank you to the people I have met
their thoughtfulness and caring are things I can't forget
most times it just costs nothing, but always leaves me touched
you say I've been like that for ages it hasn't changed me much

It makes me feel so warm inside, when people show concern
and humble too, and really hope that their respect I earn
I certainly cannot explain how on earth it's done
in general I like people and have a bit of fun.

Sometimes it's at their expense and sometimes it's at mine
I think of people's feelings and just have a jolly time
mind you at times I do slip up and then it's always wise
to think my (god what have I done) then go and apologise

And if I do it honestly my conscience then is clear
so next time that I meet them we might even have a beer
everybody's different we all have our little quirks
but I find in most cases a little humour works

So thank you all you people who make me feel so good
I don't know what it is I've got, but wouldn't sell it if I could
I just know what I give out, and all the time I learn
from so many people I get a huge return

Ah Yesteryear

When I was just a little lad, no bigger than a boy like me
I had no money, not even a penny, but I'd learnt to climb a tree
To climb a tree cost nothing, the nearest shop a three-mile hike
So with empty pockets o didn't need a bike

But back then it was normal, I expected nothing more
I could get my fun when my chores were done in the great outdoors
Mind you we all lived by a code, but then it was common sense
Like laying down and rolling under, not
straddling a barbed wire fence

When I played Tarzan in the woods and went home really tired
It was expected when I returned to take wood home for the fire
Coal was too expensive for folks like us to have
And so was toilet paper for use up in the lav.

That would be torn up newspaper collected from God knows where
And when you went you had to check to make sure some was there
Because the lav was a distance away, right the way up the garden
Which was ever so nice on a dark winter's
night with a frost beginning to harden

Scary too if half way there an owl decided to hoot
You wouldn't know whether to carry on or turn around and scoot
But then of course it may just be, the decision was too late
The reason for you journey was decided by fate

We didn't have a bathroom just that loo and an old tin bath
That was put by the fire, an old black bomber with a hearth
Water was boiled in a copper and brought in by dear old mum
And when she went to get some more, she'd
say don't forget to wash you're bum

Of course we had no electrics then, it was oil lamps and candles
In little metal candlesticks with loop round little handles
We had no running water, but three hundred
yards away was a river where
We'd go and fill up churns and have a
good drink while we were there

There's not much meat on a tadpole I found,
when I occasionally scooped one up
I strained the water after that before I had a sup
Discipline was pretty strict, if you did wrong and got found out
A leather belt came into play and you began to shout

But did it do me any harm that's for other to judge
And life is certainty easier now, and I've certainly got no grudge
I'm very thankful for what I've got and that's all just because
I can remember when I was just a lad, and that's just how it was.

Alton in Tune

Well last year now is history, a new year's come around
Do we want more of the same or shall we cover new ground
Alton town is crying out for you to visit us
We don't care if you come by train, by car, by bike or bus

We'll try and make it interesting a good place to spend your dough
We know there's other places but we don't want you to go
There's lots of places here where you can shop and drink and eat
And if you feel a little tired we've put in some handy seats

The pubs are very welcoming, the shops are all polite
Some for you convenience stay open half the night
There's museums you can wander round,
and save all questions for later
Then when you get half a chance try and baffle the curator

You could then pop in the library, maybe chat up the staff
Tell them that you want a book, a book to make you laugh
They may offer to show you round to have a real good look
I don't know why they get excited, I mean
the place is crammed with books

They go from floor to ceiling, and all so neatly stacked
Some have got hard covers and some are paper backed
Yes it's surprising what is in Alton and it's not that far away
You should see the bustle and hear the sounds on market day

You may see our town crier ring his bell and cry the news
Just come here, the atmosphere might banish any blues
So there you are then, come to Alton for whatever you may seek
Find just what you're looking for then come back again next week

An autumn leaf

A leaf on falling from a tree,
Got caught up in the breeze you see
It floated this way and then that,
And finally landed on a cat

The cat was from the next door house,
It lay there dreaming of a mouse
The mouse was huge in this cats doze
So when the leaf landed on its' nose

It jumped up arched its' back and spat
It dreamt the mouse had bit him back
But finding nothing there to fight
Took off in bewildered flight

His tail strait out, his ears flat down
He sped through villages and town
Not knowing where he went, or cared
He only knew that he was scared

Then out of breath and slowing down
He never thought to look around
But he stopped his headlong flight at last
Then wondered why he'd run so fast

He slowly realised it seemed
That the mouse was just a dream
So he turned around and back he started
To the place he'd fast departed

I think that just here I ought to say
That cat he found it quite a way
But found his house was home at last
To settle down, forget the past

That headlong flight and all that grief
And all because of a falling leaf

An itch

I've got an itch across my back it nearly drives me crazy
I thought that I might have a scratch but just too darned lazy
It's just in that awkward place I cannot reach by hand
My arms are just not four-foot long I'm sure you understand

So I have this dilemma as I lay here on my bed
An itch and how to scratch it is a teaser to my head
But then I had a brainwave I should have thought of it before
I'll just get out of bed and give it hell upon the door

But then I think of doing this anti itch attack
I might then get a splinter from the door into my back
So if the itch it still persisted and then a splinter too
I would be doubly affected so what am I to do

Oh I'll just lay here itching and have a little moan
I'd get someone to help me but then I'm all alone
If I only had a walking stick or maybe just a broom
Either one rubbed down my back would end the itching soon

There is one in the kitchen but that's a mile away
I would have to get up of the bed and that would be twice today
The first time I just had to or the bed would come to grief
But this is just a simple itch I'll use will power and belief

I'll use mind over matter and if I concentrate
I know I've heard it can be done the result might just be great
I shall will the itch with all my power to move round to my belly
Then I can scratch it easy and still lay here watching telly

Autumn

The leaves they dance and swirl around
They're free at last and on the ground
The breeze it blows them with delight
A moving swarm of autumn bright

They celebrate in the breezes gentle puff
They've hung around quite long enough
The trees, they're parents now look bear
Just skeletons of wood stand there

But trees are pleased to see them go
And celebrate their freedom so
They see them dance and move away
Oh what joy to see them play?

They know their lives will soon be gone
As the season moves along
They swirl and dance and walk and run
Enjoy the wind, the rain and sun

For winter approaches and all too soon
They'll fade away in winter's gloom
Another season has come and passes
As the world turns on its' axis

Each season has its' special glory
This is just part of the autumn story
The colours, the beauty, is there to see
Natures picture for you and me.

Big lorry

Now I am a juggernaut standing proud and big
With all my accoutrements I don't give a fig
My paintworks bright and shiny and my wheels are four foot high
There's no one doesn't notice me when I go trundling by

Whenever I am on the move it's quick get out the way
I'm like four elephants with wheels on going out to play
You can hear me coming by that roaring in your ears
And when I let my klaxon go it just confirms your fears

So clear the street get out the way and let me go on through
You just stand there goggle eyed there's nothing you can do
And when I've gone don't swear at me 'cos that would be unkind
I'm not the only one you know there's another one behind

You just stand there on the pavement and wait to cross the road
I'm a very important vehicle with a very important load
Yes we're off to god knows where with god knows what's inside
My driver got us loaded up then let's away he cried

He presses all my buttons there's lots of them you know
And there's lots of little warning lights all in a row
He keeps me looking spic and span he's very proud of me
He makes shore my bits and pieces are in good condition see

So when we're out there on the road especially at nights
You should see how great I look with all my lit up lights
My chromework it is all aglow from all the lights reflected
I'm like a moving fairground I demand to be respected

Oh I know you get annoyed my driver hears you prattle
Just because when I go by all your windows rattle
And I know who gets the blame my driver has been told
That it's our fault and only us that's chewing up the roads

Well if this is so all I can say is that I am terribly sorry
What can I do with narrow roads and I'm a great big lorry
We've got to get from A to B my driver points my wheels
With me he makes his living and we can't click our heels

We have to keep things moving to deliver what people have bought
And that is all that I can do because I'm a juggernaut

Stan w

Birthday boy

What would you like for your birthday
son at the ripe old age of seven?
Coo, could I ride in a rocket dad and go right up to heaven
Oh I don't think you would like that son,
for you wouldn't need to pack
Because if you went to heaven son you wouldn't be coming back

Don't you like being here playing your football and cricket?
Has no one told you that going there is just a one way ticket?
Your only seven years old my son, to go there it's much too soon
But just you give it a year or two you may get to the moon

I know they say it's great up there, but I wouldn't be too keen
Not until I'd met someone who's actually been
Why not let's go to Disneyland and we'll, be by your side
You'll not just find a rocket, there are lots of things to ride

We can take in all the colour, the things to do and see
Have a really smashing time, you, your mum and me
Come on you're the birthday boy so what do you say
Make up your mind then son I'll book it right away

You can then meet Donald duck and Mickey mouse as well
And when you come back you'll have a story to tell
I shall tell them it's your birthday and I know just what they'll do
They'll all dance around and sing happy birthday to you.

S, W.

Black and Decker

I've got a black and Decker garden, oh
yes it's Black and Decker true
I've got all the gadgets for the garden, a
gadget for each job I need to do
From the power runs a cable
Out past the garden table

To a place where it's easy to connect
The gadget that's required
To do the job desired
Just remember to treat it with respect

I've got a strimmer for the long stuff, and a mower for the lawn
They are all heavy duty and they save a lot of brawn
I've got a cutter for lawn edges and a lawn rake for the moss
There's a clipper for the hedges, but if no a power it's a loss

Things then begin to overtake me and if it's long they go to pot
When power it forsakes me time is something I have not
So I bless it while it's present and just keep working away
While it powers all my gadgets my garden will be O.K.

I've got a digger for the borders I've got a vacuum for the car
I just switch on to order and they work, at least they have so far
They're a boon are these gadgets for the garden,
they're a boon are these gadgets for the home
And when the weather's good you'll see I'm not alone

When I look out on my garden from a window
at all that the gadgets help me do
It's amazing the achievement possible with
the gadgets, fine weather, and you
They chitter chatter buzz when they're working,
and all you have to do is guide the thing
With all these gadgets there is no excuse for shirking,
it's so easy you can both work and sing

Black and white

I was standing in my kitchen, waiting on a boiling kettle
perusing through the window the greenhouse
and garden shed of metal,
Whence there came a magpie, to land upon the shed
He flapped and slid and flapped and skid like he was on a sled

There must have been a frost that night
so the roof was covered in ice
So when he applied his landing gear the landing wasn't nice
He maybe thought (ah that looks nice, a likely place for food)
But he really gave me quite a laugh and in a joyous mood

His spindly legs were going mad they really were a blur
Mind you I keep saying "his" it could have been a "her"
It doesn't really matter, the performance was a treat
Watching that bird doing ballet just to stay upon its' feet

The flapping of its' wings to a blur of black and white
As it fought like heck to re attain the ridge
and eventually won the fight
Then it stood there looking cocky like it was meant to be
You can't kid me miss or mister magpie I saw it all you see

And you didn't find what you came for, because I saw you fly away
Oh well here's good luck to you may be another day
But thank you for the entertainment, you were unaware I know
That I was standing in my kitchen, watching
the skating magpie show

Bowls ballad

We are a village bowls club a happy bunch of souls
We do a lot of other things as well as playing bowls
As long as we enjoy it all it's legal and it's fun
The smile we have when losing gets bigger when we've won

We shake hands with opponents before and after game
And if we lose we gnash our teeth while smiling just the same
We don't warm up before a game or do any exercises
But if we lose we try and fiddle all the raffle prizes

Come rain or shine we do not mind we've got all weather green
We've even played when snowing a sight not often seen
When really bad we play indoors, we've got an indoor mat
We always curse in English, what do you think of that

It's terribly important to always be polite
Even when the score line is not looking too bright
It's wise to then remember a certain thing they say
No matter what the score line is there'll be another day, so play.

Bright side

Now I'm a happy fella and I'll tell you what to do
If you want to be happy just like me
You just keep thinking happy thoughts no matter what you do
And you will feel so happy just you see

You go out in the morning and you greet another day
A big smile upon your face and you will find
People will smile back at you as they pass on their way
A problem may be driven from their mind

They wonder what you're smiling at, it feels good to be alive
Even though the weather looks like rain
You do not let conditions make your spirits take a dive
Because you know the sun will shine again

Just think of all those people not as fortunate as you
Or imagine just how worse off you could be
Take stock of all those lovely things you know that you can do
And you'll realise you world is pretty free

Happiness is personal to each and every one
It depends on just what gives you pleasure
I am very fortunate in finding I have some
A gift against which nothing else can measure.

Broken leg

I know a man who broke a leg in three different places
Windsor, Winchester, and at Goodwood races
How he moved I do not know it was all on the same day
His work must have made him travel that's all I can say

The pain would be excruciating as he moved about
Every little movement must have made him shout
Apparently he was not so young, he was on a pension
He didn't even go and get medical attention.

He said he had to stay at work, would use some super glue
Now what an awfully terrible stupid thing to do

But then I learnt he was ok, not at all disabled
Because the leg he broke you see was on a kitchen table
His boss upon hearing of this man's mishap
Said if you're not more careful I'll be giving you the sack

I can see it was an accident it's all the same to me
Oh why not go the whole hog and break the other three.

Cardboard box

My granddad was a great big tree standing straight and tall
For years and years he stood there before his fatal fall
He was perfectly healthy born by natures law
But he became the victim of a man and his chainsaw

They cut him all to pieces and took him to a mill
Put him on a great machine and cut him smaller still
As if this wasn't bad enough the thought just makes me gulp
They took every piece of him and turned him into pulp

The next thing was extraction of the water, and with scraper
Get every little soggy drop then turned right into paper
I don't quite know how this was done, the thought it makes me sad
You have to remember that this was my granddad

The paper was distributed and used in different ways
Now it's been recycled into other things in days
Lots of it is exported in shipping from the docks
Transformed into things like me, yes I'm a cardboard box

I know that I am useful and that feeling is so good
But remember where I came from, a great tree in a wood
So next time that you use me, maybe to put a present in
Spare a thought for granddad and all my kith and kin.

Cast Off Rhubarb

Hello, why don't you notice me when you go strolling past
I know I'm not that beautiful,when did you see me last
I've been here simply ages next to the compost heap
In the corner of the garden where you let nettles creep

But now it seems I am little use my day it seems has gone
You don't have me anymore with lots of custard on
Oh I know that sometimes I can taste a little sour
But that is when you use me outside my finest hour

I should not be pulled for eating unless I am mature
My stalks a mix of green and red achieved with good manure
Which comes from the compost heap, to me it's my best friend
And you just come and pass me by, it's no use to pretend

That you remember days gone by, for medicinal uses
You'd eat a good old rhubarb pie then later make excuses
For I have helped you clean your body of excess waste
And another something else, have you forgot the taste

With me swimming in the custard mashed up or diced
Eaten after steak and kidney I would be really nice
But now I'm here forgotten, feeling lonely and forlorn
Just behind the garden shed the back end of the lawn

My great big leaves are all spread out in homage to the sun
I'll grow here proudly on my own and display to everyone
That while I am not wanted now my uses all too few
You now just take a tablet for what I once could do

But I notice too with pleasure that you don't dig me out
Have I really been forgotten or are you in some doubt
That my days are really over as I grow there at your feet
Or will you suddenly decide to rip me out
and stick me on the compost heap.

CHOO---CHOO

There was a young puffer who chugged nicely along
Feed him with coal and he'll chug you a song
He pants as he struggles to pull his own train
His breath comes in great big puffs under the strain

His wheels get a grip with a clickety clack
He's determined to get there and then to get back
A long drink he took aboard before he got started
And with green flag a-flying then he departed

Chugging away from his home heading northward
Forever onward forever forward
His great response to constant feeding
Wey up front always leading

His health maintained with regular calls
By people in oily overalls
Oiling all his moving joints
So he can move smoothly over the points

The steam builds up to give him power
So he can do various miles per hour
This so depends on the type of terrain
But fed and watered he doesn't complain

He knows very well when he gets home
They'll polish his brass and polish his chrome
Then put him back inside his shed
Make sure he's comfortably put to bed

Until tomorrow come sunshine or rain
You can bet he'll be ready to do it again
He loves his job and toots so loud
To show us all he's very proud.

Christmas Stuffing

As we drink our glass of sherry and we think of Christmas pud
The turkey and the stuffing and another
glass of sherry? Well you would
The tables laid for dinner it looks a real delight
So you have another sherry, well you might
Then out comes the turkey and veggies steaming hot.
We all take our places, oh what wine have we got.

We all tuck in and say mum cooked a smashing dinner.
And the wine we got to wash it down with really was a winner.
Then out comes the Christmas pud, you cover it with brandy.
Someone put a match to it, if you've got one handy.

What a waste of alcohol a quite expensive drink
And then you send it up in flames, well it makes you think.
But everybody has their share and all are quite content,
So – an after dinner brandy if we know where the bottle went.
You clear away the table and retire to the lounge
The brandies poured for those who want,
the bottle has been found.

Then it's after dinner chocolates and presents then to pass.
Oh that's just what I wanted, can I refill your glass.
You don't have to worry (about driving) you stay here.
I would like your opinion on this very special beer

Oh but not just yet of course, it's this I'd like to pour,
If you'd like to finish that and try this liqueur
And don't forget the fruit and nuts and, oh my goodness me,
Just look at the time, it's nearly time for tea.
Hot mince pies and Christmas cake are laid upon the table.
So everybody help yourselves as soon as you are able

Where did we put the crackers? Those pretty ones we bought.
Oh I put them on the table by that bottle of malt.
Yes I bought that as a special treat as it's Christmas day
Why don't we try a drop right now, come on what do you say

A toast unto her majesty, why shouldn't we indulge
Mind you I think I have, my waist begins to bulge,
Well now the bottles open, a night-cap before bed,
You're sure you've had enough to drink? O.K. enough said.

<u>Good night</u>

Cold Comfort

Old Jack Frost came to visit just the other day
He knew he wasn't welcome but he didn't go away
I think he must have been upset, looking for a fight
Because when I wasn't looking he attacked my water pipe

He didn't hurt me personally although I'm rather soft
The dirty rotten scoundrel went up into the loft
I wasn't even present when he did the dirty deed
He strangled a cold water pipe and made the darned thing freeze

The blighter vanished soon enough when it began to thaw
If I could just get hold of him I'd kick him out the door
The mess he caused when he was here, really hurt my feelings
The water squirted everywhere and came down with the ceiling

To clear up the mess he caused was one of sheer endurance
It was no consolation that I could claim on the insurance
I know he made some post card pictures hanging from the trees
I admired his acrobatics but he didn't have to visit me

He had no invitation I was insufficiently prepared
I did have lagging on the pipes but he just hadn't cared
Now if there was one thing I could do, and I would be delighted
I'd grab him tightly round the neck and get him extradited.

Cold weather friend

I met and made another friend one cold and wintry day
He just appeared from nowhere, he comes from far away
He's a quiet sort of chap, who never says a word
You might think that's unlikely, but I've never heard a word

It depends upon the weather, if he appears or not
He is somewhat illusive I don't see him a lot
He only stays a little while and then he goes away
But he makes so many friends, invites them out to play

People can't resist the chance to have fun with him
Always quiet, not a sound, would never cause a din
Just by simply being here makes people want to play
He creates such happy joy, yet won't prolong his stay

He doesn't have a lot of choice of when he comes or goes
He only ever visits when it's cold, and when it snows
When the weather it gets warmer, although he's been a showman
It's been another lovely visit, from a quiet friendly snowman

Credit crunch

I am very fortunate in a credit crunch
I don't owe any money so I'm not bothered much
I don't have any savings for me to worry about
And I don't have a mortgage on my little house

All I need is sustenance, my life is very slow
But it is quite full of danger no matter where I go
I must, when I am travelling keep out of people's way
I don't know the Highway Code, I can't read anyway

I'm so shy and retiring I spend a lot of time indoors
I do have one passion though, that's making shiny floors
No matter where I go I always leave a trail
And I take my house with me, that's because I am a snail

So just watch were you put your feet, don't put me under stress
My home would get demolished not just repossessed
I too would be flattened and I wouldn't find that funny
I'll concentrate on staying alive, you worry about your money.

Crier story

When I became a town crier I considered it a mission
Never ever thought that I,d be on television
I now give talks, been toastmaster and even open shops
I find it so rewarding that I hope it never stops.

It gives a lot of pleasure to the people that I see
Is it my regalia or just little old me
In a way I hope it's both and now that I appear
I'm very pleased to see you all and hope your glad I'm here

Of course it makes a difference, if when all's said and done
You come to be entertained, and you don't get any fun
I shall have failed to write a verse to really make you laugh
Usually the stuff I write is just plain daft

I don't care I write it down if I think it's funny
You never know how things turn out someone might pay money
To read the rantings of a fool, although put down in verse
Well I've got my little dreams and things could be worse.

So there.

Decisions

Shall I do it this way or shall I do it that
I suffer these dilemmas and that's a certain fact
Should I turn it upside-down or leave it as it is
Shall I turn it round a bit or just give it a miss

Now, is that really long enough or should it touch the ground
Is that colour suitable or would it be better brown
Will that now be much too long and shall I cut it down
Will it look ridiculous when I go into town?

Have I really got the time to do that today
Are they better left together or should I take one away
When it's wet it's shiny and when it's dry it's cold
Do I want it that way or do I want it looking bold

Should I put it in a box or stand it on the top
Maybe I should hang it up but then it could just drop
I don't know what to do with it but something must be done
My dilemmas are so many and they are never any fun

Indecision worries me what to do or not
And now what was I thinking? Oh hell I've clean forgot

Earth works

As I was gazing into space a shape began to change
I focused very quickly it was well within my range
It was a little pile of earth and it was erupting
Very, very slowly mind as if something was interrupting

Being a very sunny day although the air was cold
I stood there very quietly for I guessed it was a mole
Working really hard he was pushing up the earth
I wonder what in mole terms an extended tunnel is worth

And if he sold would the price be based on what he earns
Or would they do a deal like a yard of tunnel for ten worms
You have to watch them very close they work away real quiet
Where do they get the energy? Are worms their only diet

You very rarely see one they are terribly shy
They leave piles of dirt upon your lawn that's probably why
And when you investigate with a shovel in your hand
The little devils been and gone he's back in mole land

Elbow benders

Now when you think of elbow-benders what do you see?
Someone leaning on a bar well that could be me
Refreshment taken from a nice pint glass
Sitting on a barstool but I'll let that pass

Arm and elbow rising with regularity and cheer
With mouth and lips savouring a nice pint of beer
You think of turning out time and then you see them all
Walking in the road because the paths too small

They get caught in a car headlight
They sidestep very smartly and wave goodnight
If they choose the right way they all get home
But there's other elbow-benders, like the mobile phone

You see people in doorways or even pushing a pram
Elbow bent phone to ear, here I am
Of course you weren't there when the conversation started
But what is it they talk about? They've only just parted

Or you're in Sainsbury's, then what was that you said?
A jar of jam a pot of paste and a thin sliced bread
In the middle of the crowd in a world of their own
Hand to ear elbow bent mobile phone

Excuse me did you say something? Were you talking to me?
Then you spot bent elbow, and present apology
Or you're standing in the post office nice orderly queue.
And suddenly the strange sound, and they all think it's you

But then they see bent elbow that gives away the culprit
And they aren't embarrassed are they but why do they do it?
You go into a restaurant for a lovely meal to scoff
And there you are bent elbow why can't they turn it off?

Envelopes with windows in

At first I hear a car door slam, then footsteps on the drive
The rattle of the letterbox, the postman has arrived
I contain my excitement and quickly don my togs
And go to see just what is there, oh no, more catalogues

Surely in between them there must be something more
Something really interesting worth walking to the door
And then I spot an envelope anticipation grows
I see it's got a window in, oh no it's one of those

They never bring excitement or set the pulses soaring
It doesn't matter what's inside, it's always pretty boring
I know it's all-official stuff, maybe forms to fill in
My very first reaction is to toss it in the bin

But I mustn't do that, it's official I must cope
Why don't they fool us with a coloured envelope?
Keep the contents hidden till the very last second
I would look forward to the postman even more I reckon

Then when it was opened to find what was within
It could be from the lottery to inform you of a win
It could be from anyone with that envelope
Oh no it's from the tax man, oh well there's always hope.

Expenses

Oh I'd like to have a job that paid expenses,
not to boost my salary you understand
But to cover, what I call essentials that I have to settle out of hand
Not to break the law of course that would be pure deceit
And I would back up every claim with a good valid receipt

A job which meant some meetings in cities or towns abroad
Where I had to go on business that my firm could well afford
A hotel for a night or two with all my comforts found
And on return submit my claim for every blinking pound

Then of course there's corporate lunches and entertaining guests
My much needed laundry for my pants, socks, shirts and vests
I have to look my best of course to represent my firm
So all that would have to come on top of what I earn

And when I'm away a lot I would need a second home
A company car a brief case and a mobile phone
I would need to show my status as long as I kept the rules
And I would claim the mortgage too, life would be so cool

I'd care not that the rules were daft, I would claim my whack
And I would sue them if they tried to give me the sack
You know I've just this minute realised the job that would suit me
I'll go and buy a pin stripe suit and become a new M.P.

Fairies

They say there's lights out in my garden and
there's fairies down the bottom
Now I knew about the lights of course, but
fairies? I didn't know I'd got'em
Do they really play on toadstools because that's what I've been told
And would I dare question it ? Could I be that bold?

Or am I so blind and cannot see the things others accept
Or is it just a fairy tale as I really suspect
I have seen many toadstools at the bottom of the trees
But I've never seen little people living there happily

And if they really are there where do they go during the day?
Or do they go where all the lights go? Because they all go away
I know the lights are solar are the fairies too
Have you seen the little people ? If so what did you do?

I would like to believe it, it's such a lovely thought
But when I go down the garden all I see is nought
I check round all the toadstools and really stay alert
But after all my efforts all I find is dirt.

Health and safety

When in the past I have considered health and
safety and found that if I lived by all the rules
The things I did would take me ten times longer
and need a massive shed for all the extra tools
Then security would be needed for the contents and the shed
There would be so much worry I'd be scared to leave my bed

But to lay there without sustenance how long could I fare
Then to brave the kitchen and it's dangers, well
just think health and safety would I dare
I think of all the things that just might happen
as I prepare a meal ore cup of tea
So I don protective clothing to cook the meal and take care of me

And then things could get hot, as I turn the
cooker on and then get steaming
As from the cookbook and my mind a lovely meal I'm dreaming
So I stand there safety helmet, eye goggles and gloves
Try to get the joint out of the oven, and
spuds in boiling fat in tray above

Tell me how I get the joint out of the oven wearing
boxing gloves and steamed up goggles
And however did we get along without them?
When I think back my mind just boggles
So I say let's forget this health and safety and
then we can relax and not be tense
We should go back to how it used to be and
just rely on good old common sense

How Santa

Father Christmas poor old chap we just take him for granted
He tries to get us everything that we have always wanted
But just how does he manage it he only works one day
Does he have a boss and get holidays with pay

Just how does he do it, with his reindeer sleigh and sack?
Hardly has he started out when he's got to be getting back
And all those chimneys in between, and he's always merry
Mind you that's understandable with all that cooking sherry

But how does he manage it? How does he find his way?
Has he got a sat nav mounted on his sleigh?
I wonder, if he did get lost who would he ask
I have so many questions, and for him what a task

He doesn't even have a mate just to lend a hand
Just him and his reindeer a perfect one man band
And he never seems to age at all he always looks the same
I don't what it is he takes but I wouldn't mind some of the same

Unless of course the medication gives you all that hair
Then I think I shall pass on that, I'd rather have my chin bare
You see there's all these questions I keep asking in my mind
A plea, is their someone out there with answers I could find?

Hygiene

When I think of personal hygiene I find it quite amusing
The sequence of ones actions is terribly confusing
I make use of the toilet and a sign before my
eyes says now wash your hands
So should one wash them straight away I don't quite understand

If you wash them straight away your clothes still round your feet
Then shuffle to the wash basin with others to compete
Stand in line to wait your turn clothes dragging the floor
Until your hands are nice and clean, then
adjust your clothes once more

Or do you first adjust your clothes your hands of coarse unclean
And so transfer any germs to clothes (see what I mean)
I have to smile to think of gentlemen all standing in line
Clothes around their ankles just the same as mine

And then of course ones clothes will pick up germs from of the floor
So one will have to wash ones flipping hands once more
Now I am all for hygiene we really must be clean
But life's so complicated and now we are going green.

In the wind (a mounted knight in shining armour)

I had a mishap coming here today and the storey I must tell
My horse stumbled and through me off and guess in what I fell

With a hey nonny nonny nonny no,

I tried to rise and slipped again just to make the job complete
Twice more I fell thrice more I rose which left me on my feet
Then I caught my horse and remounted of
coarse to continue my journey here
But everyone was warned of my approach of that you need not fear

With a hey nonny, nonny, nonny, no

The wind you see was following me and bearing the news ahead
So everyone was warned of my approach of this need more be said
Of this of course I did not think it had not crossed my mind
That if you wanted good clean air you had to be behind

With a hey nonny, nonny, nonny, no

Then did I chance to come upon a maid so fair and sweet?
I bade her to accompany me, she said not even from fifty feet
Forsooth you mind fate is unkind, and my journeys yet to end
A wandering minstrel bade me good day
then vanished round the bend

With a hey nonny, nonny, nonny, no

Me thinks I need to make more speed because I am unclean
I'd been in it right up to here and not fit to be seen
So I arrived at the castle gate to meet the local gentry
They lowered the flag down to half-mast and then refused me entry

With a hey nonny, nonny, nonny, no

Now as befits a gentleman I enquired of their wishes
They said you swim across the lake and don't disturb the fishes
Now I must admit it did the trick, my embarrassment washed away
I stand before you fresh and clean and care not what you say

With a hey nonny, nonny, nonny, no.

It was me

It was me who through the wellie in your fish pond, it
was me who ditched the beer cans in the hedge
It was me who chucked the gravel at your window
when you was tucked up nicely in your bed
It was me who made the racket that woke up all your
kids and then you couldn't get them back to sleep
I grinned when you was angry and raised your voice
you see, cause I was by then laughing in the street

I like to make you wonder who's doing all these
things when I rings your bell and runs away
I never care about the damage that I cause,
I know it isn't me who's got to pay
I'm not bothered I'm a nuisance, I like a bit of fun at your expense
Last time that I went by I was feeling rather high,
so I tipped next doors dustbin over your fence

I smiled when I thought of you next morning,
when you found the mess upon your lawn
And I just bet you'd like to get your own back,
well your too late cause I'm long gone
I don't what to do tomorrow maybe I'll spray paint all up a wall
Just so long as you know I'm still around
and oh boy I have myself a ball

First I drink a can or three and then I have some fun
I get to boast to all my friends the things that I have done
Maybe they've all done it too, were all vandals you see
Were the ones you talk about, we make you so angry

To us it's just a laugh you see and should you call the police
Well even if they catch us. We shall soon be all released
They might give us an ASBO or fine us a few quid
But it would have been worth it for the fun and things we did

We don't know why you kick up such a fuss,
we have been pampered and adored
But now we have grown up a bit we find we get so bored
And we don't know what else to do, I suppose this is our hobby
To be a vandal is our game, to frustrate you
and the local bobby (ha ha ha).

It's crackers

I'm always in my party dress just waiting for the call
at the end of every year ready to give my all
I lay there waiting patiently and cannot make a sound
there's twelve in my family and all are duty bound

All of us are colourful and all are slim at waist
we're always very popular and appeal to every taste
when we are called to do our bit it really is such fun
but we only get to do it once yes only just the one

Because we know when we go out we won't be coming back
our dresses will be torn to shreds and enthusiasm lack
and then amid the merriment our insides will reveal
a trinket and a paper hat the trinket won't be real

So now we've served our purpose relegated to the bin
once more we meet the family but what a state we're in
dishevelled, screwed up, thrown away pulled by separate hands
that's the life that we all live, here in cracker land.

It's modern medicine

Modern day medicine is something to behold
It's not until you're ill do these wonders unfold
When they want to take your temperature nowadays I hear
They say turn your head sideways then stick this gadget in your ear

You only hear it ding twice then it's over and done
A far cry from the days when they stuck
the thermometer up your bum
But this is quick and sterile that must be pretty plain
But when first done to me I thought gee, the insertion of a brain

Then the search for blood pressure, a never ending quest
They wait until you nod off then interrupt your rest
They bind your arm then blow it up, by compressor if you please
It gets tighter and tighter until blimey what a squeeze

You think your arm will just drop off then the motor it cuts out
I think it's mental torture that's what it's about
And then you see a nurse with tray, in the background linger
Then before you know what's up she stabs you in the finger

I only want a spot of blood it's not spectacular
Wasn't that what someone said of count Dracula?
She doesn't use a needle oh no this little gun
It's modern technology it's where they get their fun

But they still need a sample that's altered not one jot
There's bottles still about the place filled up with you know what
For all these modern gadgets hanging from the walls
It's still a human in the bed and that's when nature calls.

I've been pulled

I'm always in my party dress waiting for the call
Ready when needed to go and give my all
I lay there waiting patiently and cannot make a sound
There's twelve of us in my family and all are duty bound

All of us are colourful with slim and wistful wastes
Reared and presented to appeal to every of taste
When we are called upon to do our bit for fun
We just get one performance, one, and only one.

When we are called we know full well, we won't be going back
Our dresses will be torn to shreds, our voices made to crack
And then amid the merriment, from inside our very heart
From All our worldly possessions, we are made to part

By then we've served our purpose, where're discarded to the bin
And there is all the family but what a state were in
Dishevelled, screwed up, thrown away, all pulled by different hands
And that's the short life we all live, in Christmas cracker land.

I've seen the light

My garden's full of little lights all powered by the sun
It's my dear wife who put them there, yes every blinking one
I don't know why she put them there she doesn't weed at night
Perhaps she wants to stand inside and watch some hedgehogs fight

But then there are no hedgehogs there as far as I can tell
And so the mystery thickens, a case on which to dwell
Perhaps she's made some secret plans of which I do not know
Maybe she's got a contract to extend the runway at Heathrow

But nothing yet has landed, come roaring from the sky
Well that is only two blackbirds a robin and magpie
Mind you that were in daylight when the lights they are not on
When do they go off anyway? Do they know when it's dawn?

It's not that they are a nuisance, and it's not that they are glary
But do you think it could possibly be a theme park for fairies
So I asked my wife what were they for?
And just what was their price
She said oh they were very cheap and I just think they're nice.

I'm a connoisseur of jumble sales

I'm a connoisseur of jumble sales, that's those occasions when
you gather bits and pieces from relatives and friends
it comes in bags and boxes or sometimes it comes loose
from boots and shoes to camping gear and maybe a plastic goose

There's puzzles and a painting set underneath that book
Oh, a day with Fanny Cradock well that might please some cook
and there's the doorbell once again some more has just arrived
hang on please I'll just shift this there's still some room inside

The sale day fast approaches and the house is getting smaller
to see out of my window now I need to be taller
mind you if you've experienced this as often as me
you'll know by now I've forgotten where the furniture should be

It really doesn't matter, it won't be for long
I've said that so many times it could almost be a song
the phone rings but where is it? Oh it's just behind that box
completely covered over by a dozen pairs of socks

I lift the receiver and I hear this lady say
I'll drop some jumble in your porch I'm coming by your way
I thank her very much and say I'll be glad if she would
she says it's nice to know it might do somebody some good

And so you come to jumble day with quite a lot so far
and once more you wonder will we get it in the car
you get the car out ready all the doors are open wide
and all hands available start packing stuff inside

You don't think it's going to work but you don't bet on it
while cramming so much in the boot it
may be coming out the bonnet
oh well that's the lot just this thing for cutting meat
and there's a little bit of room underneath my seat

Now squeeze it jam the door shut there's nothing now we lack
Oh dear that's not very nice that handle in my back
so here we are then at the hall let's get this lot in
just mind you don't spill all those buttons from that tin

We sort it all out to what goes where
is there another one of those to make a pair
there's toys and games and clothes untold
don't take off your coat it might get sold

Now we're all ready so open the door
10p each to come in that will be a few pounds more
now it's all hustle they push and they shove
turn everything over for that other glove

They find it and offer a whole 2p
you banter and barter and end up with three
their hand dives into a very nice coat
then they say "can you change a five pound note"

You dive for change all fumbling haste
selling time's precious, too precious to waste
there's a ten pence piece in an outstretched hand
in payment for a lovely fan

And so it comes in small amounts
but it does come and that's what counts
10p buys a shovel with a broken handle
now don't forget your tickets for the raffle

The stock goes down the pence pile up
that's about it, it's time for a cup
the raffles drawn, they take their prize
then depart leaving chaos before your eyes

You count the cash your glad you did it
although the hall looks like a bomb had hit it
all hands wade in and you get cleared up
then maybe have another cup

Get all washed up floor swept with broom
hall gets locked up then off home
sits at table well that's that done
I quite enjoyed that, where's the next one.

Limericks and things

There was a young man from Medstead
Who invented a real woollen bed
But he got agitated and really frustrated
When the sheep it was on went and fled

An old man from our club one day went
To a brewery to see beer ferment
He said well now that I'm here
Let's see all this beer
Then fell into the whey and away he went

Words are a way of expressing oneself
They are formed by the mouth and the tongue
Some words are beautiful lovely and nice
Some words are ugly like bung

If railway trains were candy floss
And lines were liquorice sticks
If all the men were marzipan
And the women chocolate dips
Signal boxes lollipops how easy it would make
A smashing railway system we could lick them into shape

A man of a delicate age, fancied a job on the stage
He didn't know what, but he found that he'd got
No agent, no prospect, no wage

Limericks

There was a young man from Devizes

Whose legs were two different sizes
He was shocked when he found
Only one touched the ground
But at hopscotch he won all the prizes

A young man I met from Killkady
Four times he was a daddy
With four different ladies
He fathered these babies
He kept loving and leaving did Paddy

Me and my computer

Me and my computer are not the best of pals
it makes me so frustrated I keep chewing on my nails

I use the mouse, I use the keys and follow what it says
but nearly every blessed time we both go different ways

I sit here quite determined to bring it into line
but after half an hour or more it's all been wasted time

My head is full of icons now what does that one mean?
if we could work together we might become a team

What the devil did I touch? Something happened on the screen
what was it? And where did it go? Or was it just a dream

I'm sure I just saw something move or do my eyes deceive?
I don't trust my computer, it's against me I believe

But I am so determined to make things come out right
I must not let it beat me, I'll continue with the fight

I'll try this, I'll try that and see what happens then
I'm sure I did it right that time, it would be quicker with a pen

Ah I know what I'll do. I'll check back in the book
that should tell me what I need, I'll have a little look

Oh, it says here — but I have just done that
I think where I went wrong was when I came in here and sat

But there it is it's my fault, I went and switched it on
I think I'll give it up for now so where's the off switch gone?

Medieval Knight

Before it got dark I was a medieval day, but now I'm a medieval knight
With my armour all shiny and clanky and new I'll bet I don't half look a sight.
But I'm brave and ferocious and I serve the king I've got his best interests at heart.
Besides if I don't he gets really mad and says you and your head could soon part,

Then from down on my knees I'd say majesty please all us knights are with you as one,
And then he would say in his own funny way, all right I know you've just had your hair done.
It's not always easy being a knight, it's not all wine women and song
You've always got to be in the right even when you're in the wrong.

The king one-day he summoned me and bade me go to the wars
He sent me off with greatest speed, then called me back for my horse
My horse he must be five foot high, he might be even larger
I call him battery because of his shape, he looks like a battery charger

But he's healthy and willing and gets me about, but the ladies all see me and scoff.
I try to ignore them, I ride on before them, then damn me I go and fall off.
A peasant you see then says unto me, can I be of assistance my lord
And me with no choice says in a high voice, help me up man I'm sat on my sword.

This armour is ever so heavy you know, we ride with great difficulty
I once saw another great knight fall off, mind you he was eighty three.
Now my sword's a formidable weapon, sharp, and as heavy as lead
In combat one swish, my opponent says missed, and I say try shaking
your head.

For entertainment we have banquets once or twice a year
We sit on wooden benches, and grab the serving wenches, as they try
and keep our goblets full of beer.
So when we've eaten enough and drunk enough the minstrels start
to play.
Then we cavort about the place, getting in each other's way

And it can be very painful, especially on the feet
If you go and tread upon, a bone you've thrown there from the meat
Such a stupid habit, we should really try and stop
Throwing bones over the shoulder not caring where they drop

Still, it's the serfs who do the clearing up we would not soil our hands
It's knights and earls who do the fighting in the promised lands
So wherever there is trouble, wherever there is strife
The king he always sends for me, I wish he'd send for the wife.

So sayeth it remindeth me when I left home she begs
Journey homeward early Sir Knight, I need your hat to boil eggs.

Mr Blackbird

Hello Mr Blackbird what are you doing then?
Were you pecking at my seeds, well don't do it again
You go out and have a hunt in the farmer's field
I'm sure you'll find enough out there to make a three course meal

Those seeds they cost me quite a lot in town the other day
So don't you look at me so sad, you go on, go away
I do not wish you any harm, I wish you all the best
And if you like you're welcome to use my hedgerow for your nest

But that doesn't mean free bed and board, I like my garden clean
Not bits and pieces scattered round, you know what I mean
You get your beak in everywhere, on you it doesn't dawn
That on your frantic search for food, you mess up my lawn

Now when you raise your family with all those mouths to feed
There's plenty of food just over there in amongst the weed
But if by chance a juicy worm should pop up from my ground
Feel free to take advantage but don't leave mess around

And teach your little fledglings as they are growing up
That I am not a takeaway, a supplier of quick grub
So spread your wings and look about don't just rely on me
There are other people's gardens, some with feeders in a tree

My pet hate

I once decided that I would sit down and write
and tell you about something I really do not like
or even better still a statement I would make
about a certain thing I really, really hate

And that is garlic, and I find it really rough
to know that some people even eat the stuff
it smells revolting and tastes just as bad
then as soon as consumed it repeats like mad

It can be smelt from yards away
and still be detected after a day
who was it, I wonder in days gone by
that was desperate enough to give it a try

Were they starving or just plain mad
how ever could anything taste so bad
it stays forever on the breath
to a relationship could be the kiss of death

I have found out from experience
that we don't always check ingredients
you eat something and it tastes just swell
then you're told that your breath does smell

You find the empty carton or maybe the tin
then say "oh damn" it's had garlic in
now if I could find a food inspector
would he have a garlic detector?

Have they been invented yet? Is that what he would say perhaps I could invent one, that would make my day they would sell in their thousands, with instructions how to correctly use them, I'll go and invent one now.

OH YEZ---OH YEZ---OH YES

Names like George, Fred and Harry,
Bill and James are great

Sound like good old English names, and popular to date

But this young George is special, a Royal prince No less

Another member to our royal family,
for which we should be blest

He was born so young and as yet he knows not why

But in the future folks will bow to him
a young man born so high

We shall watch his progress as he grows with lots

of fun. So I say god bless him and
his father and his mum

GOD SAVE THE QUEEN

No voice

A town crier I know lost his voice
He found he had so little choice

He then wrote a sonnet
Spent lots of time on it

Then burnt it on legal advice

Not yew tree me tree

If I was a tree I'd stand up tall no matter what my age
A sapling or an English oak or could be a greengage
I'd be brave with my branches and raise them to the sky
And if somebody messed with me I'd poke them in the eye

I'd make my leaves all shiny to attract the birds and bees
And I'd also make them slippery so they didn't mess on me
They'd slide off then and go away and little insects too
I wouldn't let them mess with me I'd think of things to do

They might just pass me a disease with operation urgent
Then my health is in the hands of a qualified tree surgeon
Oh yes I'd have it all worked out I wouldn't just stand there mute
I think my biggest defence is to stand there looking cute

But possibly needed at my base some nice sharp pegs
So I could get my own back when doggies cock their legs
And then of course there's termites that could get inside my skin
I would have to think of something to stop them getting in

Perhaps I'd let my sap leak out and seep all down my trunk
So they would get their feet all sticky and want to do a bunk
I'd want to be a shapely tree and be much admired
So they wouldn't want to cut me down to burn me on the fire

I would spread my branches wisely and they'd see what I had made
A lovely place to get their chairs and sit under my shade
I would protect them from the sun if it became too hot
And they could shelter from the rain if that is what they'd got

I would really be so useful they wouldn't want me gone
I would even let the little ones my branches swing upon
The only trouble is that many people do not think
They come and tack things on your trunk as quickly as a wink

They use those things called drawing pins or could be a staple gun
It does hurt I can tell you but you can't get up and run
Yes I would provide a service I think you would agree
I'd stand there proud and swaying in the breeze you see a tree

Nudists birthday

What do you give a nudist when her birthday comes along?
Maybe you could give her a kiss and sing her a birthday song
You could always wish her all the breast
and admire her birthday suit
It's no good giving her money she's nowhere to put the loot

You couldn't give her an accordion the squeeze would be a pain
I think she'd only use it once, she wouldn't do that again
The folds in the accordion would make her eyes go runny
And I don't really think she would find that very funny

You could give her a nice iced lolly, that's maybe to her taste
But she wouldn't want to drop any, she would lick with undue haste
Would you wish her welcome and acting very bold?
Offer her a seat making sure it wasn't cold

Or she would stand up quickly and rub her chilly cheeks
And say your hospitality is the worst she's had for weeks
So what would you give a nudist when her birthday comes along?
I'd give her a great big cuddle now don't you get me wrong.

Oh blow it

There's something I've been looking at for literally years
It's something situated between and forward of my ears
It gets no fertiliser but that's where it grows
The thing I'm referring to is my own large nose

One possible advantage of this I think I've found
That if I fell forward my face would not touch the ground
I'd be saved by this appendage so prominent and big
But if it was on soft ground a nice hole it would dig

I'll try not to think of it that would be a pain
And while in good condition it does divert the rain
Also in summer it provides a lot of shade
It saves my lips from chapping from the heat the sun has made

It does collect the lovely smells that in the air abound
The trouble is it smells the others to when they're around
But where would I lodge my spectacles if I didn't have a nose
They would have to redesign the glasses I suppose

But there's a thing I think about that really tickles me
That I didn't have a nose I maybe couldn't see
But just to smell those fish and chips I think you'll, all agree
How very important a decent nose can be

But when we evaluate all the buts and ifs
We don't value our hooter when we get the sniffs
And have to keep wiping it, we have a cold or more
Then you find the next thing is the blinking thing gets sore

You walk around with a conk like a Belisha beacon
On top of that of course the darned thing won't stop leaking
But when it's fully functional I'm happy I suppose
That mostly I get good clean country air up my great big nose

OH YEZ---OH YEZ---OH YEZ

The day maybe chilly, it maybe wet
May not be welcome, but it's what we get
Just two people or lots together
Why do we always talk of the weather?

Never predictable it's hot, cold, or it blows
I know not whence it comes but know where some goes
It's draughty, uncomfortable, not all the time
Sometimes can be pleasantly warm

Where're an island affected by the Gulf Stream and such
So whatever we do we can't alter much
I don't know I'd want to, it's OK by me
I quite like not knowing, the uncertainty

So let's stop our moaning, enjoy what we've, got
We're all here and free in this beautiful spot.

GOD SAVE THE QUEEN

OH YEZ-------OH YEZ-------OH YEZ

Yeovil

Alton, Hampshire, great market town countryside setting,
green fields for a gown
Come tourists visit us, yes have a ball
We're very friendly, and welcoming all

Check the steam trains, on the watercress line
Visit Jane Austin's house, and Gilbert Whites that's fine
Learn about fanny Adams, visit the grave
A horrible crime but it did coin a phrase

Learn of the battle in sixteen forty three
Musket ball marks on church door still to see.
A high street with shops in fine architecture
With side streets beckoning tourist with camera

Scars can still be seen in the church where it ended
A Colonel Boles killed, Alton he defended.

GOD SAVE THE QUEEN

Oh yez---oh yez---oh yez

The Olympics

The opening and closing what a show
How we beat that I do not know
To keep it simple may be best
We've nothing to prove to all the rest

Our athletes made me very proud
I want to cry their achievements loud
They went to Beijing and gave their all
Of medals they made quite a hall

I applaud their efforts, their dedication
Everyone deserves an ovation
Their courage, and good old British grit
Made me watch spellbound I must admit

2012, London, bring it on
Four years I know but ding-Dong

God Save the Queen

OUR CARIBBEAN CRUSE
(or talk at the table)

There was one named Peter and one named John
With Pat and Jill, June and Chris what a carry on
We would all meet for dinner at the forty-seven table
Then try to rise when finished, that's if we were able

The conversation wavered on topics this and that
As we waded through the menu which really suited Pat
But he looked at me and with a disapproving frown
Said you can't order yet Stan you've got the menu upside down

In a while my order came and June would
say (Stan what have you got there)
And I would look at Jill and Chris and my
dear wife Kath as they did stare
I can't say that I recognised my order on the plate
But they all knew I had ordered it so most of it I ate

I do say most of it, because it's shelf life I did doubt
Because the starters and the main course seemed to be growing out
There was little sprouts of greenery, it's garnish I was told
To make the dish look pretty and to make your taste buds unfold

And so dear friends I write this ode to tell you straight from me
What really made our holiday was your great company
The food was good and entertainment too,
but what really was a winner
At six fifteen, table forty seven when we all met for dinner

And to you ladies thank you, although we met by chance
You took my hand and chanced your arm
when I asked you for a dance
AH all those memories we all have to treasure
So thank you all just once again it really was a pleasure

Pawn broker

If I were a pawnbroker I would break a lot of pawns
I would break some in the afternoon and the some in the morn
I would break one when I fancied and if I had one to spare
I would take it out and with a hammer break in anywhere

I wouldn't care just where it was, I wouldn't care who saw
Because to break the pawns you know is not against the law
Only when you've done it and you leave a mess behind
Then of course if you get caught you face a hefty fine

But pawn broking is not messy and I would like to try
To make it very popular so folks would want to buy
And then when it was popular I would gather all statistics
Then in a year or two I would enter the Olympics

But I don't know who makes the pawns or where you get them from
I thought I saw one in a shop but when I checked it had gone
So to anybody out there would you kindly do your best
Find me a pawn maker to satisfy my quest

Yes find me a pawn maker with pawns that I could break
I do not mind what size they are any would be great
Except if they were massive or way over the top
Because if I were successful I might open a shop

I could then have balls upon a pole a symbol of my trade
I don't know where I would get the balls
but I could have some made
But then why balls I ask myself that idea seems daft
I must concentrate my mind I could sell it as a craft.

Pet Hate

I decided to sit down and write
About something that I do not like
Or better still a statement I will make
About something that I really hate

And that is garlic, and I find it tough
To understand people who even eat the stuff
It smells revolting it tastes as bad
And when consumed repeats like mad

It can be smelt from yards away
And still be detected the following day
Who was it I wonder in days gone by
That was desperate enough to give it a try

Were they starving or just plain mad
However could anything taste so bad
It stays forever on the breath
To a relationship could be the kiss of death

I have found out from experience
We don't always check ingredients
You eat something and it tastes just swell
Then your told your breath does smell

You find the empty carton or maybe tin
Then say oh dam it's got garlic in
Now if I could find a food inspector
Would he have a garlic detector?

Have they been invented yet I wonder by the way
Perhaps I could invent one, what would garlic haters say?
They should sell in their thousands and make me a rich man
I know I can do it, at least - I think I can. ----------We shall see.

Pigeon love

I was sitting in my conservatory reading a book
I heard a scuffle in the trees so I had to have a look
I wondered what the heck it was, I guessed it was a bird
But it wasn't just the one or two, I found there was a third

They were skittering and flapping and jumping at one another
All pigeons look alike to me I can't tell one from the other
For that's what it was you see making all that noise
It must have been a pigeon girl besieged by pigeon boys

And then I realised of course that we were into spring
The pigeon boys were up there trying to mate like anything
By the way they were acting I could tell which was the female one
And she was playing them a merry dance she was having fun

First she would reject the one, and then the other one the same
But they'd keep trying it on she was driving them insane
Then as I kept watching they both followed her in flight
To carry on their love making in another tree, well they might.

Potholes

As the owner of a tarmac drive I felt a bit left out
I hadn't got a pothole like all the roads about
So I looked in yellow pages to see where they were made
Obviously they didn't put any in my drive when it was laid

There must have been a reason for not having them I suppose
But if so why do we have them in all our roads
So I thought that I would have some only two or three
Then placed an order and awaited delivery

They came in a lorry with a great big crane
I fancied that was so they could be lifted in and out again
But the driver said it didn't work the thing it had had its' day
So why don't you take it off it's only in the way

He said hold on I'm not the boss I only drive the lorry
alright mate I understand I said no offence I'm sorry
And so he dropped the tailboard and to tip them he'd begun
But as they slid down to the ground they all joined up as one

A dirty great big pothole the site just made me wince
Worse still the driver then reversed and we haven't seen him since
I rang the firm to tell them just what had occurred
But they just would not believe me they said it was absurd

Why would they not believe me why would I tell a lie
So I told them it's the last pothole from you I'll buy
Now if you should come to visit me be careful don't fall in
My dirty great big pothole before I fill it in

I've gone off the idea.

Published

I would very much like my poems to be published
I know not everyone thinks they're rubbish
Of course I would have to make it right
To protect my copyright

And to be sure that they would earn
A very just and fair return
For those involved in the project
Then surely no one would object

From me the author to the person who buys
All should gain in various ways
They certainly shouldn't bring on the blues
Indeed I hope they will amuse

Puddles

I would like to export puddles to counties who have not
Got very little water they are just too flipping hot
It should be a good earner the demand should be great
Those people must be boiling, how do they concentrate

What sort of water should I use cloudy or clean
Should it be straight out the tap or get it from a stream
How would they use my puddles then I have to think
Would they paddle in them or use them just to drink

And then of course there's transport to places way out back
I suppose I could wrap them in a bubble pack
That would stop them slopping over when they were in transit
And could be stacked one on the other in spaces made to fit

Ah now something I've just thought of about the bubble pack
Will they get the water out the front or out the back
And where will they put it when they get it out
Do they have spare potholes just lying about

Or maybe I could sell a package pothole with puddle
for the DIY trade so they won't get in a muddle
I'll have to do some research and find out all I can
And then sit down and get drawn up a proper business plan

If I could catch some water every time it rains
And store it temporarily before it goes down the drain
Then when my production line is all up and running
The factory can still be working even if it's sunny

This is such a good idea I wonder more and more
Why has no one ever thought of it before
Perhaps they did think of it but to do it didn't dare
But I reckon by this time next year I'll be a millionaire

Reflections

Now as I look in the mirror and I see me looking back
I say to my reflection why didn't the mirror crack
I see this great big nose and then I see the grin
And then I think what sort of state is that face getting in

Of course it's getting older, wiser too I like to think
One can see it in the eyebrows and the way the eyelids blink
I can see it in the wrinkles and in the sagging chin
And gaps are in between the teeth and the hair is getting thin

The forehead's getting larger than it used to be
Can the bloke that's looking back really be me
It's just not right, life really is not fair
It gives you wrinkles and takes away your hair

It makes you ache both knee and back
It makes your skin go dry and crack
Move quick, work hard, it makes you pant
Things you could do now you can't

Your tennis elbow hurts like mad
The frozen shoulder's just as bad
The swelling in your leg's gone down
But fallen arches now you've found

Your ingrowing toenails too are a pest
The pain when you walk demands that you rest
Your eyesight too seems to be failing
You no longer can see from what you're ailing

Is there something from which you lack?
Could you be a hypochondriac?
You're sure you're in for a touch of flu
For goodness sake what's got into you?

Stop all this fretting and self-inflicted strife
Get out there and give yourself a life
Try to stop worrying about what you've got
And thank the world for the ills you've not

Rejected

It's not nice being lonely and find you're being shunned
But that is what my life's been like and it isn't any fun
I don't know why I'm so disliked I've done nothing wrong
It doesn't matter where I am. I feel I don't belong

When little children meet me, they push me to one side
The fact is their dislike of me they really cannot hide
I'm green and round and harmless I am no threat at all
The grown-ups too are choosy, when their eyes on me do fall

I really do feel rotten the way I'm treated so
If I had legs I'd walk right out, just get up and go
But every time that I appear, I am singled out
Rejected, pushed to one side because I'm a Brussel sprout.

Remember ?

Oh I wish I could remember the faces that I see
I know, I know the people but their names escape me
I puzzle who it is when they say, "How are you Stan"
Why can I not recall their names when they know who I am?

They say, "that was good the other day" now I need time to think
What are they referring to, my mind is on the blink
Where were we together and what was the event
I just hope they will drop a hint that would be heaven sent

The things that happened yesteryear I all too well remember
But for things so much more recent I must consult the calendar
What is it about the brain that plays these dirty tricks?
Where recall fails but sometime later out of the blue it clicks

It's too late then the moment's past, and times moved on since then
I went to town the other day and it happened once again
I know I met old, what's his name? Once lived just up our road
On hearing news he always uttered (well I'm blowed)

Years ago played football, played a fair old game
Oh it doesn't matter I can't recall his name
Does this affect all my age? Have we been singled out?
Partial loss of memory as well as having gout

My train of thought goes back and forth, now what have I forgot?
How am I to end these verses? I've gone and lost the plot
I really have to ask myself am I going round the bend?
While I've still got my faculties I shall call this "the end"

Scarecrow

I wouldn't like to be a scarecrow, a very lonely task
No I wouldn't like to be one, so you needn't even ask
Just think what doing that all day, really does involve
Standing in one place in rain and storm and cold

Silent and on their own, they stand out in a field
Put there by the farmer to protect his harvest yield
Doomed to be a bachelor and frighten birds away
He leaves them out there all the time and they don't get any pay

And when the birdies fly around and go down for the seed
Feel sorry for the scarecrow, it must make his heart bleed
He cannot shout or move about to do his job correct
So if the farmer loses seed what can he expect

Why not make the scarecrow mobile, and give him voice to shout
The birds they would all scatter then and screech what's that about
But as it is, so static, no company, food or drink
A horrible occupation, the poor chap can't even blink

And when the harvest is gathered in at the end of the season
If the yield is down for whatever the reason
The farmer looks round for something to blame
And I'll bet he blames the scarecrow, what a blinking shame.

Shadow

I am a grey patch on the floor or maybe on the wall
Sometimes I'm quite tiny and sometimes ten foot tall
Sometimes I'm in front of you, sometimes I'm round the back
You simply can't get rid of me, redundancy or sack

I do have a dependency, which is I must have light
And you can't move without me, forwards, backwards left or right
Where're you go then I go too, we just cannot be parted
It's no good running, I will be there the same time you've departed

Accept the fact that I'm friendly, wouldn't hurt you if I could
I'm your life long buddy that should be understood
You don't have any option, there is no other choice
One thing you should be thankful for, is I don't have a voice

I'm not your conscience or your guide, but if you move I'll follow
I'm just that dark patch you can see, yes I am your shadow.

Silent town crier

Mr town crier you're quiet, do you have no news to give out?
You're not in your usual regalia why so do I find you without
have you done something wrong and become a disgrace?
It won't be the same without you round the place

We're all pleased to see you when you do your rounds
We know you're about when we hear the bell sound
But you're here and you're silent I want to know why
I've met a town crier that hasn't a cry

Please answer me sir you're looking so down
When you ought to be ringing, crying and waking the town
Is it something I've said sir? Won't you answer me back?
Is it deafness from ringing the bell or have you got the sack?

What's that you said? Would you say it
again? I'm afraid I didn't quite hear
If it's personal or private it won't be repeated
of that you need have no fear
I don't understand, I think you said you
wanted to stand where the light is,
Oh, what an utter fool I am, you said you've got laryngitis

Snowflake

As I float gently down to ground with millions of my mates
a tiny little snowflake and we will congregate
yes, when and as we reach the ground, we will join together
just tiny little particles all formed by the weather

And as we lay upon the ground, a blanket pure and white
humans roll us into balls and have a snowball fight
and when they get fed up with that, they roll us even bigger
they make us into snowmen, a sort of human figure

Little branches from the trees become arms both left and right
they get two pebbles from the road as if to give us sight
a length of cloth goes round our neck which they call a scarf
they then stand back, admire their work and have a jolly laugh

You've put my eyes in all skew whiff, I know your hands are cold
I need a nose so I might sniff, and don't make me look too old
a mouth is realistic too, though I shan't make a sound
a hat too is sensible with all those birds around

Ah ha so now you've finished me, you're proud of me no doubt
and the weather is improving, the sun is coming out
now I don't like the sun at all, it is no friend of mine
all the time it's cold and crisp my life is really fine

But now it's getting warmer, I start to melt and shrink
all my bits start falling off, almost quicker than a blink
and before you know it, with not one tiny falter
I disappear before your very eyes, turned right back into water.

Spring

Now the sun is shining. The bulbs are coming through
there's lots and lots of snowdrops and crocuses mauve and blue
the grass it just looks greener and buds begin to show
the world seems to be waking up, lets hope there's no more snow.

The weather just seems all amiss it keeps nature in doubt
it knows not when to stay asleep or start it's coming out
is it us that's mucked it up with progress made too soon
with chemicals and rockets and travel to the moon.

If it is, where will it end? With floods out in the desert
sandstorms in our cities, the reverse of the world's weather
I don't suppose I'll ever know, but it really makes me think
what is the world coming to? I think I'll have a drink.

That man

I wonder how he does it? I'd find out if I could
He doesn't have a website so that's no blinking good
He never ever seems to age, not like you and me
Every time I see him he's the same exactly.

He never seem to shave or have his haircut back and sides
But he's always clean and tidy and regularly rides
He never smokes and doesn't drink as far as I can tell
And he's always happy, bright as a new brass bell.

He never seems to change his clothes he always wears the same
He never handles money so what's his little game
We don't see him very often; he travels far and near
Yet everybody knows him that is pretty clear

He's pretty good with animals and little children too
They look forward to his coming and know just what to do.
We would all feel left out if he went and missed us
I refer of course to the man himself, yes it's Father Christmas.

Stan W

The bottom of my garden

There are fairies at the bottom of my garden
Down where the rhubarb used to be
And that's the stuff that made me beg your pardon
Because rhubarb disagrees with me

The fairies used to like it or so I do believe
Because I was always finding little nibbles in the leaves
I also liked it very much but should really go without
The health and safety side of things I will not write about

The fairies are not very pleased of that I have no doubt
I must have made them angry when I pulled the rhubarb out
I didn't see a toadstool ring or any sign of life
Her indoors would think me batty, no I won't tell the wife

I'm sure they now play tricks on me they didn't play before
Now when I have a bonfire they blow the smoke next door
And so I have to put it out and try again next week
I wonder if there's such a time when fairies go to sleep

They wait until I mow the lawn and then the leaves they scatter
I cannot see the rascals, but I hear their pitter-patter
Or is it my imagination and just a fantasy
I think I'll give the garden up, and go and watch TV.

The club

I belong to a club, a club for the over forties (ahem)
It's called the Alton health and fun and it's really sporty
Some say we are the wrinklees and are over the hill
It could be true that most of us are on some sort of pill

It could be that one is for the onset of gout
Though you wouldn't know it the way we rush about
The flash of table tennis bats are completely a blur
That if you get a rally going amid the laughter

It gets really competitive you really try to win
That's if you cut the cackle and actually begin
The queue for play is large with everybody able
And they've all just come from keep fit to try and get a table

The agility is something else in the midst of battle
And afterwards there's always gossip and tittle-tattle
There's also bowls and badminton and table tennis too
It's much more fun than sitting home wondering what to do

It's best to just get out there and have bit of fun
There's always a smarty pants to show you how it's done
Forget your fallen arches and that rash upon your belly
And all those operations that you've seen on the telly

Just get out there and play something, just go and do your best
And if you get a little warm strip off show us your string vest
We don't care we'll have a laugh and you will laugh as well
Just grab you racket, bat ore bowl and say what the hell

We may be getting on in years but we aren't dead just yet
When we do feel poorly then it's the doctor ore perhaps the vet
And when there you bare your chest and he applies the stethoscope
Then says your tickers going strong, oh yes you've still got hope

You then replace your clothing thinking he is very kind
And make a hasty exit in case he changes his mind
So you then go back to the club feeling better to
And everyone says welcome back come and join the queue.

The dentist

My wife went to the dentist his name was Mr Heath
Which is so convenient because it rhymes with teeth
Easy to remember when at him you'd like to swear
You can't of course your mouths agape with dentist's tools in there

Why do dentists talk to you when your mouth is open wide?
Sometimes they make you think they're trying to climb inside
He knows you can't reply as you gaze into his eyes
He's got you at his mercy, I wonder does he hypnotise

All these things run through your head, but I think you might agree
I hate the flipping dentist, well perhaps he don't like me
But you're so defenceless when you're sitting in his chair
You can't protest he's got you and to move you just don't dare

It doesn't really hurt these days, at least that's what he said
But there's one hell of a racket going on in your head
There's whineing and grinding, you can feel his breath (it's hot)
But when it comes to it what choices have you got

Your teeth have been aching bad and you've been in such pain
And then he says now rinse and spit, oh that routine again
Last time I sat up and spat as quickly as a wink
And then he said disgustingly no not there in the sink

Now I'm getting past the point where I really care
I just do heavy breathing and wish to god I wasn't there
I'm sure you will agree it just isn't any fun
Then glory be the man just said okay you're done

Whew

The flea

I know that I'm an irritant and get right in your hair
But I'm like you I'm full of life and have to live somewhere
Oh know please don't scratch like that, you get me in a pickle
I have to move about to feed, and that's what makes you tickle

I'm sorry that I make you itch it isn't my intent
But until I satisfy my hunger I cannot be content
I have to search among the hairs all over your head
And if I'm not as quick as you I could end up dead

Mind you I'm pretty nippy I need to be you see
We have a reputation in the guild of busy fleas
Once a week a competition, on the best to irritate
I've won it twice, not on your head but the head of your mate

His head is much cleaner, a better place to eat
Not a varied menu and there isn't any sweet
But I love a nice clean scalp, or other feeding grounds
The trouble is you always seem to know when I'm around

I never really get the chance to make stable home
It's only too often you bring out that blinking comb
That's when I need to hop it quick onto pastures new
But when you least expect me, I'll be back and bring my crew

The Gazunder

Has anyone got a gazunder? Or some people called it a Poe
But it used to be called a gazunder because under the bed it would go
And quite a fitting name I think, it described the thing just right
The thing, oh such a simple thing that saved us miles at night

In years gone by at dead of night clutching torch or candle
And feeling great discomfort as you fumbled for door handle
Opened the outside door and oh good heavens it was chilly
But you had to endure it to try and reach the privy

Privy was another word, what we now call the loo
But when you're really desperate there's little else to do
And that was up the garden, and a very draughty shed
A bucket and no water and somewhere to bump your head

An owl may hoot or other sounds tests the courage you may lack
It would be terrible going up, but not so bad going back
Returning to the house, wash hands, water freezing cold
To visit the toilet in those days you just had to be bold

And so we blessed the gazunder it saved us quite a trek
Sometimes going up that path, well you could break your neck
But use of the gazunder gave us great relief
And unlocked privy up the garden?, well we never had a thief

The only things to pinch up there was newspaper or bucket
So we reckoned anyone would be really desperate to take it
Privacy was maintained by foot against the door
Or if one heard footsteps you whistled no need for more

Unless you had a thunder box emitting sound effects
Telling it was occupied of that you could detect
Then you had a problem, just what are you to do
The answer to this question I leave entirely to you

The ladies loo

Something that perplexes me I don't know about you
Is women's strange behaviour when visiting the loo?
They never seem to go alone there's always more than one
Is it some sort of tribal thing? Long ago begun

They always take their handbags swinging from their arm
Do they take that as a weapon should they come to any harm?
But what harm could they come to in such a busy place
Ore are the handbags full of makeup to retouch the face

Is there another reason of which we shouldn't know?
To always be accompanied when they've got to go
Do they need assistance to fulfil their endeavour?
So they take some friends along to do ------- whatever

Do they take the opportunity maybe while they wash their hands?
Handbags swinging from their wrist then drying under fans
To talk about their ailments and what a time it takes
It all remains a mystery and I daren't investigate

To me a man it's out of bounds and I cannot intrude
It would be bad manners and considered very rude
It's private just for ladies so perhaps then from now on
I shall mind my own darned business and just carry on

The limes

Well another week has passed and here we are again
Soaking up the sunshine and soaking up the rain
But we don't care where, now inside and in our usual chair
We're once more in the limes centre where everybody cares

We look to left and right to check that everybody's here
And if there's someone missing we ask if they are feeling queer
But with luck we find we all are tickety boo
Except for him and her and her and him and her and you

But we won't take any notice they just want sympathy
Do you know we've been here ages where is our cup of tea
We all have our priorities our cup of chars a must
But the staff are all so very kind we don't like to make a fuss

No they do look after us and see were entertained
And if the standards terrible we know just who's to blame
But while where're doing this our minds are off our troubles
And if we please the staff we might even get a cuddle

They've not got any favourites they treat us all the same
And they won't tell us any smutty jokes isn't that a shame?
Still we do like coming here for friendship and a meal
And it's filled another day, the entertainment's real

As three o'clock approaches and the mini bus has come
To take us all back home again, we've had a bit of fun
Oh don't forget your walking stick, or you're walking frame
Ta-ta everybody we will see you all again.

The mole

I'm a furry little fellow with a pointed nose
No one seems to like me wherever I may go
Yet I travel in silence and never make a sound
Only travel slowly but I do get around

I never trouble anyone im terribly shy
To put me in the limelight I'd really rather die
I'm usually working in a dark and very confined space
I really cannot figure out why I'm in disgrace

You very rarely see me so it cannot be my looks
You may have only seen me as a picture in your books
If I chance to visit your place you might not even know
Unless you also chance to see some little earthworks grow

But by then I'd probably have gone to pastures new
Because once I've well worked one patch there's nothing left to do
I never ask for much in life just enough to eat
That's why I keep busy just underneath your feet

So next time you see signs of me don't get mad, come to terms
With the fact that all I want is lots and lots of worms.

The popular pigeon

I am a wood pigeon sitting in a tree
eyeing up your garden to see just what's for me
I see you've been so busy pulling up the weeds
when are you going to start planting seeds

Then I will just wait for you to go indoors
And that's when I shall swoop down and pinch what is yours
Please don't plant them too deep or I shall have to scratch around
You know you get excited when you find iI'veve been around

I shall scratch out your beetroot carrots and peas
And you'll be down there cursing me underneath my tree
Oh I can here you mumbling from up here where I sit
Because I don't care what you plant I shall have some of it

And when you plant your cabbage plants you do give me a treat
Rows and rows of lovely greens just right for me to eat
I have to look out for the cat he's always after me
I've just got to be alert and whisk straight up in my tree

And I sit there all cheeky like he doesn't stand a chance
I fly right down and up again I lead him quite a dance
Until my crop is all full up then I fly home to bed
And coos and caws over my mate who's sitting on the eggs

We do this twice or more a year that's how us pigeons breed
And that is why we raid your gardens for a good old feed
So the next time you curse me im just doing my best
To raise my little family back home at the nest

I know you also get upset at the marks I leave behind
But we all have to go somewhere so don't be so unkind
It's not nice to be unwanted and always shooed away
You should try and be a pigeon just for a day.

Town crier

Now I am town crier with my big loud sponsored bell
Sponsored regalia and spectacles as well
My body isn't sponsored as far as I can tell

I roam the streets of Alton both to the north and south
With my parchment with my cry-in and my great big mouth
Telling people of the town just what is on and where
Where to go on Saturday to buy their Christmas fayre

The council write my cry you know and tell me what to say
And I had my picture in the herald the other day
People like to see me as I proudly stroll along
I try to make them realise they really do belong

To a town that does its' best, some people really try
To make it a good place to live, to trade to sell and buy
It sometimes takes a lot of time, to make things come to pass
Only six shopping days to go so I wish you a Merry Christmas.

Waffle

One of the things I do in life when I am sat at home
Is put pen to paper and write some sort of poem
I just get the urge to write and make things up to rhyme
But there is no telling when it's the right time

It's just when words and circumstances enter my head
So sometimes have to write it quick before I go to bed
Because if I don't do it quick the moments thought has gone
Then how can I continue? I just cannot carry on

The driving force within me for better or for worse
Keeps pushing my excitement to finish the blinking verse
I'm not sure where it's going when I first begin
I just have to let it out from somewhere within

The subject can be anything serious or daft
I wonder if anyone might consider it a craft
Like painting a picture or working with wood
If someone enjoys reading it that's got to be good

The trouble is that's sometimes like right now
I can't think how to finish it somehow
I wish I hadn't started now it was just a passing thought
All these words I've written and I feel I've achieved nought

Sometimes it's quite enough to drive me round the bend
Ah that's it I've done it because that rhymes with end (whew)

When I was born

When I was born I'm told my mother said to dad
Alright I've had enough that's five boys I've had
I love them all but misbehave they get me in a whirl
Oh why couldn't I just this once have had a little girl

Anyway she looked at me then turned me north then south
Knew that I was hungry but she couldn't find my mouth
She wanted to breast feed me and I kicked up such a din
So that she would know which end to put the nipple in

I was always hungry and on mum I could depend
Especially when I was uncomfortable at the other end
She tried to rear me into a man she could admire
I wish you could se me now mum I've become a town crier

It was all that bawling when I was a kid
Especially when I got a cuff for all things I did
They was never nasty things, just things they thought was naughty
But they taught me to be pretty good and now I'm way past forty.

Why

I know it seems a waste of time to think of days gone by
But I'll ask you all to stop a while and ask the reason why
Why don't people sing now or whistle in the street
And if they did we,d look at them as if they were,t complete

Should we blame the telly or the juke box in the pub
Or are we all too busy just trying to earn our grub
I know that life is hectic and some things have gone wrong
But would it help a little if we all burst into song

I know it must be difficult for the kids as well as me
They used to sing a song of sixpence now it's two and a half pe
Our postman used to whistle when he brought the morning post
And sometimes he might stop awhile for a cup of tea and toast

And when he'd gone we,d all feel just a little better
But now of course it costs a bomb just to post a letter
We used to have a sing song down the pub on a Saturday night
In some pubs now they,l say that's enough of that allright

The good old sally army they seem a happy lot
They sing their hyms out on the street and give it all they've got
So if your in the doctors surgery on a bus or in a queue
Why don't you just burst into song and the best of luck to you.

Winter

As I look out of my window and I see the pouring rain
I wonder if we ever will see the sun again
There's a lake over my garden there's a river in the street
There's water everywhere you look the sky has got a leak

I think about the birdies who do not choose to sing
I think about the little moles and all tunnel living things
They do not have umbrellas or little plastic macs
They cannot seal their tunnels the earth is full of cracks

The water all comes dripping through their homes begin to fill
Do they all then emigrate to the nearest highest hill
But I have never seen a hill its' summit full of creatures
Way above the waterline with their survival teachers

So I look out of my window my thoughts are all aflow
And so I just console myself I just don't know.

Work

I'm sitting in my garden shed looking at the rain
thinking about those little jobs I cannot do again
I could not do them yesterday and with little sorrow
all things being equal, I won't do them tomorrow

They just seem to taunt me but I will not give in
to get struck down with gardening would be a mortal sin
once the bug gets hold of you wherever will it end
if you're not very careful you'll be finding things to mend

Then it's pinch your finger time or go and bump your head
I find it so much safer to stay inside my shed
I can look at the lawn mower wipe off the nice clean paint
think about starting it then decide against

That was a close call I nearly dropped my guard
work came creeping up on me I must concentrate hard
I look at all those shiny tools for garden and for lawn
then I have another look and stifle a yawn

I used to grow vegetables, oh there's the garden line
well that is all behind me now I'll have a glass of wine
I keep a bottle in the shed only just the one
just in case I think of work and then get overcome

It doesn't happen often only once an hour
but it does help a little to boost my will power
if I got tempted out there it would really be a shame
because between me and nature there's this little game

She will just keep tempting me to do this and that
I think about it briefly then turn her down flat
the trouble is she's crafty with really cunning ways
she'll tempt you out and beckon you with warm and sunny days

But I must be strong and concentrate. Repeat inside my head
no matter how she tempts me I must stay inside my shed
for I must remember when all is said and done
to be free of the infection I might be the only one

WWW. Potholes. Com.uk

To write about traffic calming just now is my goal
For those of us in Hampshire it's known as the pothole
What/ you say you haven't got any, oh you come from surrey
Well if you want to be like us you'd better hurry

We have limited stocks of most sizes and shapes
A simple invoice what you want is all it takes
It can be next day delivery in flat packs while stocks last
All the larger sizes and deep one's going fast

We do take orders for specials made to measure
And a pothole bulk purchase price always a pleasure
We mould with best tarmac then take away the skin
Which leaves a lovely pothole for car wheels to drop in

Of course this has been patented to protect our design
But if you want a franchise at a price that's fine
We do have ones especially designed for a bend
So they can't complete a turn without a suspension to mend

As a traffic calming measure nothing can compare
With this potty pothole system designed with skill and care
We regret we can't take old ones in part exchange
We suggest you re site them in some quiet country lane

We do offer supply and fit if that's what you desire
Professionally sited in the way of every tyre
If you would like to view our work before you place an order
Then venture into Hampshire, come across the border

We know when you've inspected the potholes we've installed
And you've dropped into one or two our future is assured
A new factory is on cards to keep up with demand
Our salesmen say large orders are on the way we understand

A recruitment drive for pothole makers we have underway
Our target for production is five thousand a day
Transport is no problem, thousands fit inside a van
The colour range is limited to just black or tan

Now this is quite intentional our design team is slick
Any other colour drivers would spot to quick
A web site will be set up in the middle of a field
With catalogues and advertising all will be revealed

Our materials are imported with quality control
Space comes from the space centre at cape Canaveral
Every pothole has the kite mark the British standard sign
So you know you get the best when you purchase some of mine

A problem in production that we have found so far
Is that when we take the mould off we don't know where they are
But that's a minor problem and we shall soon put it right
So tell me sir or madam how many would you like

Lightning Source UK Ltd.
Milton Keynes UK
UKHW011907080120
356600UK00002B/85/P